# THE LITTLE BOOK

# OF

# FARTS & POOS

## (And other Bits and Bobs of News)

### By

### A. P. Hart

Published by
HART

British Library Cataloguing-in-Publication Data.
A catalogue record for this book is available
from the British Library.

ISBN 978-0-9930117-0-2
Printed in Great Britain by
Arthur H. Stockwell Ltd
Torrs Park    Ilfracombe
Devon  EX34 8BA

# CONTENTS

I welcome you to this book,
Please come and join me – take a look.

# INTRODUCTION

There are many claims to fame when it comes to fart records. One such achievement was apparently noted back in June 2006 where the fart lasted a remarkable two minutes and forty-two seconds! It is alleged that this record still stands.

So, the question is, are you up for the challenge, could you make it into the record books?

## Good Luck!

## Explanatory Notes

It is a little known fact that F.A.R.T. is actually an acronym for the phrase Force Air Rear-end Turbo. Likewise, P.I.S.S. is an acronym and stands for Persistent Irrigation System Solutions. M.A.F.F. – Ministry of Agriculture Food and Fisheries – now D.E.F.R.A.

I hope this helps.

# A FART TO BE PROUD OF

Well, what are you waiting for, now is your chance,
To break this record with one of your farts.

So sit down quietly, all other thoughts barred
When you feel one coming just squeeze really hard.

Now brace yourselves chaps for what's coming next,
There's a distant rumble – it could be a jet.

Oh my goodness, it's gone really dark,
The windows are rattling, it sounds like a fart!

Please hurry, take cover, there's one coming through
And they're usually followed by low-flying poo!

Oh my word, well that one was strong,
And at **two minutes sixty** – incredibly long!

So well done you, you **are** number one,
We were sorry to hear that it scorched your bum!

But we've been trained, we know what to do,
With a quick blast of foam you'll be good as new!

# BICARBONATE OF SODA

Sprinkle this around the loo
After you have had a poo.
It will keep the smells at bay,
And even make them go away!

Pheweee!!!!

# A DIETER'S DILEMMA

My friend Sue's done so well
She's given up smoking and drinking as well.

But now she's trying to lose some weight
She's got herself into a bit of a state.

She's spent hours and hours at the local gym,
No matter how hard she tries she just cannot get slim.

She's tried swimming and rowing, the art of kung fu,
Skipping and dancing and dieting too.

But alas, nothing works, she's just getting bigger,
So why is this happening to her lovely figure?

But all is not lost here's what I suggest,
And if this doesn't work then you tried your best.

You've given it your all Sue, right from the start,
Perhaps all you need is a bloody good fart!

## THE APERITIF
### How do you like yours?

Some like 'em hot, some like 'em cold.
Some like 'em young, some like 'em old.

Some like a double, some like a short.
Some would be in trouble if they ever got caught!

Some like 'em rough, some like 'em smooth.
Some have got taste, while others could improve.

Some like 'em cheap, some like 'em dear.
Some like to choose a particular year.

Some like 'em fruity, some like 'em plain,
And some will drink anything and never complain!

# ONE TOO MANY!

My friend Jan's not so well
And when you see her you can tell.

Her arm's all swollen, red and raw
And when you poke it, it's very sore!

We're very sorry to hear of your plight,
But you must put more tonic in your gin at night.

We've told you before about drinking it neat.
If only you'd listened, you'd have stayed on your feet.

But there it is, the damage is done.
If you do it again, try and land on your bum!

# THE JOYS OF . . .?
## (Oh dear! – Do you know, I just can't remember!)

It really is quite odd and I find it very strange,
That as I'm getting older there are many things that change.

I tend to lose my memory and things just disappear.
I know I put them somewhere, but where is so unclear.

You won't believe the things I've lost, never to be found.
Where they go I just don't know, it's really quite profound.

And my eyes don't seem to focus like they used to do.
So now I'm wearing glasses with built-in hearing too.

My skin is not so supple and the wrinkles start to show.
No matter how much cream I use, I've lost that youthful glow.

Memories they are so vague, it really is just weird.
I'm sure that when I was a girl I didn't have a beard!

And when I look into the mirror, it gives me such a fright.
'Cos the stranger staring back at me is such a scary sight!

But where will it all end? It frightens me to think.
So, I'm popping to the loo to cause yet another stink!!!!!


PHEWeeeeeeeee !!!

## IS THERE ANYTHING THAT YOU FORGOT TO DO THIS MORNING BEFORE GOING OUT?

You get that awful feeling, you just know that something's wrong,
When you find yourself in town and you've got your slippers on!

You see the crowds all turn and then they stop and stare,
So you check you've put your teeth in and that you've combed your hair.

Then – **OH, SHOCK, HORROR!** There's toothpaste round your lips,
Your knickers are on backwards and your trousers are unzipped!!!

Then you wake up with a start, let out a piercing scream,
To find that all is normal – that it was just another dream!

# IF I HAD A MEMORY

If I had a memory,
I wouldn't be so slim.
I'd be on different diets
And going to the gym!

But as it is I haven't,
I'm always in a spin.
Once around my bowl
And I've forgotten everything!

# THE ICE-CREAM MAN!

She's so easily pleased and she doesn't ask for much,
Just to have an ice-cream van that turns up after lunch.

It's about that time of day, you see, when she gets rather peckish
And without an ice to quench her thirst she can become quite reckless.

She hears the chimes of the van, like a calling from the wild,
Then leaves her desk and runs outside as if she were a child.

You often see her in the square, mostly in the summer.
But the way she chases after him, it so does not become her!

As she sprints across the street, arms and legs akimbo,
The little man he speeds away, one eye in his rear window!

So who is this woman? Tell me, what's her name?
Is she that crazy lady of West Country fame?

Oh yes, it's Ali from the office, but there's no cause for alarm.
Just buy her a '99' – and she'll remain quite calm!

# MIDDLE-AGED MAN IN LYCRA

Now, Danny has a problem you cannot clearly see,
It lies below his waistline, but well above his knee.

It comes from pedalling much too hard out on his brand-new bike,
Or perhaps it is quite simply that his Lycra's far too tight!

We know the reason why he's been looking oh so glum.
It's really very simple, it's the soreness of his bum!

As he pedals up the hills and down the other side,
He struggles and struggles with all his might to satisfy his pride.

But it's no good, his body's weak, his legs begin to falter.
He wobbles, flips and loops the loop and ends up in the water!

As he floats around the dock in a horrid soggy state,
He hopes that someone will rescue him before it's all too late.

Then in the distance there's a whirring sound, it looks like Frank the crane.
He hooks him up and winches him out and leaves him there to drain.

When he comes round there isn't a sound, just the faces of Frank and Bill,
All tear-stained and red and shaking their heads –
"Oh Danny, you do look ill!"

You'll be glad to hear that Danny survived and has finally sold his bike.
The only surge he gets these days is surfing Internet sites!

# GNOME WITH NO 'OME

Gerome Gnome hasn't got an 'ome,
He relies on you and I
To keep him fed and watered
And full of shepherd's pie!

He's very partial don't you know,
To wine and a little cheese.
And if there were some sloe gin,
He'd weaken at the knees!

This isn't a one-way friendship
As it would seem right from the start.
'Cos if you squeezed him gently,
I'm sure you'd make him fart!!!

# ARE YOU WORMAPHOBIC?

I am a little worm,
And I wiggle to and fro.
How I make you scream that loud,
I really do not know.

I know that you don't like me,
I think that I can tell,
'Cos when you catch a glimpse of me
I hear you shout and yell!

"Help, help – he's back again
It's that horrid little worm.
Can't you keep him out of here,
He makes my stomach squirm."

But I'm only small, I mean no harm.
Please, don't turn me away.
I promise to stop scaring you,
Please, will you let me stay?

I'll live down in your bin
And I'll do as I am told.
I'll eat up all the waste you bring
And turn it into 'gold'.

And when you see your plants in bloom
Please spare a thought for me.
I'm that 'horrid little worm'
That you couldn't bear to see!

# TWO LITTLE SUNFLOWERS

Two little sunflowers sitting in a row,
One is growing quickly, the other rather slow.

They're in a race you see, who can grow the most.
All eyes are on the finish for the first one past the post!

The little chap he tried so hard to be upright and tall,
But there were days when he found, he couldn't grow at all.

So he looked up and told his friend, "I want to be like you."
"It's really very simple son, 'cos I'm just fed on poo!"

# THE FLIRT

Kirstie! You are a flirt,
There can be no denying.
And now you're not content with that
On **my** boys you've been spying!

I've seen you lure them in,
And cast them under your spell.
Haven't you got enough of your own,
Without nicking mine as well?

I only used to get a few,
Two or three times a day.
And now to get them over here,
I find I have to pay!

I can't compete with what's on offer,
The wit, the boobs, the fun.
Now I'm just an afterthought,
With my tiny little bum!!!!

# WEDDING BELLS

Dear Dan and Nicky
I send good wishes to you,
For all of your life
And in all that you do.

Marriage is a partnership
Both equal and fair,
The good and the bad bits
There to be shared.

There's one thing, Dan,
To remember if you can,
That Nick's senior gopher
And you're right-hand man!

So now I've got that one
Out of the way,
I wish you love, health and happiness,
For all of your days.

# I'M A HOUSEWIFE – GET ME OUT OF HERE!

I really don't like housework,
It's all I seem to do.
I begin on Saturday mornings
And start by cleaning the loo.

I do some washing, make us lunch,
Clean bedrooms one and two.
But I really don't like housework,
And it's all I seem to do.

I clean the lounge, we walk the dogs,
In that there's nothing new.
Then I do the ironing
And clean the kitchen through.

But I really don't like housework,
And it's all I seem to do.
I really, really need a break,
Why can't you help me too?

Weekends are very short,
They always seem the same.
Before you know, it's Monday
And I'm off to work again!

Why don't they hear my cries of help?
I've made it very clear.
I'm not just a housewife,
**Please, get me out of here!**

But if there is an afterlife
My plans are all pre-laid.
I'm returning as the laird,
And not that poor old maid!

# A DOG'S DAILY JOG!
## (Boris is a sprightly Jack Russell)

The name's Boris and did you know, I'm a sporty little chap?
Each day I sprint around the park and then I sprint right back.

I go with my friend Ben, he lives with me you know,
But there are days when he can be oh so very slow.

It's stiffness in his knees, or so he's telling me.
But I think it's very simple, he just likes the sympathy.

Well I don't like the rain, I'm always getting soaked!
I think that what I really need's a little doggy coat.

It's on days like this that Ben will say to me,
"We'll pop out quickly for a poo and then a little pee."

But I can't just go to order, I'll see what I can do.
The bit I find most tricky's that elusive little poo!

# COWBOY BUILDERS!

This is a tale about our loo,
You need to take heed this could happen to you.

The builders came to strip back the wood,
To replace the tiles and make it look good.

To change the basin and renew the loo,
To upgrade the lights and the flooring too.

But it's a mess I'm afraid to say,
It looks so bad we're refusing to pay!

There's paint on here, there's paint on there,
In fact, there's paint just everywhere!

The tiles aren't straight, the toilet's broke,
Flush the loo and you'll get bloody soaked!

It's hard to believe skilled men have done this,
It's just like someone's been taking the piss!

So, who is this builder, what is his name?
It must be a firm of considerable fame!

It's 'Bodge-It and Leg-It', didn't you know,
Please **don't** be tempted to give them a go!

# BACK TROUBLE

'Poor old' Kim's not so well
And when you see her you can tell.

She's all bent over to the knee
And not up straight like you and me.

Life's really hard when you're bent in two
Especially the times when you need the loo.

You can't stand up, you can't sit down.
You jiggle around like a circus clown.

Then you finally make it and things seem OK
'Til your back goes **crack** and you're there to stay.

As you sit there and ponder what you should do,
Out pops a fart and a lump of poo!

It was such a good blast, just what you need,
'Cos you're back on your feet and finally freed.

# REGGIE'S LITTLE PROBLEM!

Now, Reggie has a problem you cannot clearly see,
It lies below his waistline, but well above his knee.

It comes from falling from his bike *fart-too* many times,
And when he sits down it's plain to see there's tears in his eyes.

We know the reason why he's been looking oh so glum.
It's really very simple, it's the soreness of his bum!

There is an easy way to solve poor Reggie's plight.
Perhaps he might try walking or converting to a trike!

# THE HEAT PAD

Now, if you're sore or feeling poorly, heat up this little pad
Then wrap your arms around it, it'll stop you feeling sad.

Then close your eyes and dream away for however long it takes,
And you will feel much better by the time that you're awake.

# BERTIE THE BUG
**(Bertie and his friends are just three fun-loving
little grain weevils playing in a grain store)**

Bertie the bug was a right little thug, just like his friends Rue and Dill,
He was older than them, reached the grand age of ten when suddenly he fell
ill.

They were playing one day in a heap of corn, when Bertie espied a large tin,
He levered the lid and was looking inside when suddenly he fell in.

It was full of powder with a terrible 'owder, he struggled but couldn't get out,
No matter how hard he tried he was stuck inside, so he started to scream
and shout.

As he lay there all limp and feeling quite sick, he wondered what was his fate,
He prayed that someone would rescue him before it was all too late.

Then all of a sudden there was an almighty bang and into the air he flew,
In all the commotion he got out of the tin, quite how he never knew.

When he came round there wasn't a sound, just the faces of Rue and Dill,
All tear-stained and red and shaking their heads – oh Bertie you do look ill.

You'll be pleased to know that Bertie survived and now has a walking stick,
As he hobbles around on five legs all day instead of the statutory six!

# THE COMMITTEE GIRLS

You're the girls behind the scenes who make the wheels go round
And when there are some funds to raise you're always to be found.

Rushing here and rushing there, there's so much to be done.
So much to get organized before we have our fun.

There's the hall to book, things to sell and prizes to be found,
And then there's all the adverts to get us folk around.

And when the day draws to its close and we have all gone home,
There's you and Noel left behind to clear up on your own.

You've done your duty and served us well from toddler through to school,
But now the local comp has shut there's not much more to do.

And so now the time has finally come to say a fond farewell,
Please raise your glasses in a toast – **To Jenny and Noel!**

There's one more thing before I go that I'd like to suggest,
That you and Noel take a break and have a well-earned rest!

**CHEERS!**

Why is that when local authorities need to save money they seem to want to do away with the things most dear to us. On this occasion it was the lollipop lady.

## THE LOLLIPOP LADY

So come everybody
This has got to stop.
We must all stick together
To save our lollipop!

We'll call on health and safety
See what they have to say,
I don't think they will like it,
And our lollipop must stay.

Do you have to take such risks
To save this paltry sum?
Can't we think of something else,
That won't cause so much harm?

Written for those who get a thrill from being out on their bikes at night with no lights on!

# BE VISIBLE

Do you have a death wish?
You gave me such a fright
To find you out there on your bikes,
In the dead of night!

Without a light between you
You really must be mad!
There could be so much carnage
And that would be so sad.

So lights on please and let's be seen,
That's all you have to do.
It would be much safer
For the likes of me and you.

# TO THE PHANTOM FORK NICKER!

We used to have some forks,
They were in our kitchen drawer.
But when I looked the other day,
They weren't there any more!

Could you say you've seen them
Or you know just where they are?
Are they outside in a van,
A truck, or company car?

And how they came to be there,
We'd really like to know.
Could you help us track them down
And fetch the blighters home!

Do you have a fetish,
That you'd like to share with us?
Is there something deep and secret
We really should discuss?

Do you like to hoard things
And stash them all away?
Do you like to save them
For that 'rainy' day?

If this is you, your game is up
It's time that you came clean.
Please bring them back and wash them up,
You're being very mean.

It's bloody hard to eat your lunch
With just a kitchen knife.
Come back here without them
There could be trouble in your life!

# SANTA'S LITTLE HELPER

Oh Nicky what have you got?
You really don't look well!
Your ears have both gone pointed
And you've grown a beard as well!

There's a wart right on your chin
And a huge one on your nose
And when we turn the lights off
That's the one that glows!

It's such a strange phenomenon
That's very rarely seen.
Perhaps it is an omen,
We must find out what it means. . . .

Well, it seems that you've been chosen
By Santa Claus himself,
To help with Christmas duties
Along with all the elves.

You'll keep a watchful eye
As the kids go to and fro,
And if they have been naughty.
Then you'll let Santa know.

So come on all you children,
You better had be good.
'Cos you won't get any presents
And there'll be no Christmas pud!

# THE ELUSIVE BALLPOINT PENS!

I've always found it strange
And I don't understand,
How when you need a ballpoint pen
There's never one to hand.

It's always been the same,
They seem to disappear.
Where they go, no one knows,
It's never been that clear.

You can see where they have been.
There're tops gnawed and chewed,
But you rarely find a whole one.
I'm totally confused.

We often get together
And try to round them up.
But they're really quite elusive
And we don't have too much luck.

We find tops without bottoms
And bottoms without tops,
So when you're done, please leave them whole
And put them in the box.

Then they're there for next time,
We'll be saving money too.
Perhaps we'll get enough put by
To have a treat or two!

# A BEAR'S DILEMMA
**(Written for my niece and her lifelong companion Jerry Bear,
who both went off to university last year)**

My name is Jerry and as you know I'm an educated chap.
I've travelled right way round the world and then I've travelled back!

And now I'm off to uni, my future's in my paws,
I know that if I study hard it could open many doors.

I'm really worried about leaving home and being on my own,
So I'm taking my friend Penny, so I won't be all alone.

My bags are packed and ready to go, I've taken all I dare.
There's only one thing left to ask – what should a young bear wear?

# COLD CALLERS

Sir, I thank you for your brilliant verse.
I accept your apology for being so terse.

But to say "Go away", I thought too polite,
You must try harder, put up more of a fight!

Just say "Bog off", now you've gone too far.
We've got double glazing and we don't have a car!

And, if you haven't got the message, I'll make it quite clear,
We don't need your help – just stop calling here!!!

# THE FINANCIAL ADVISORS

My name's Danny and this is Shane
Financial planning's the name of our game.

We're very good at what we do,
And we're here right now to share this with you.

Our service to you will be tailor-made,
To fit just like a suit that's been handmade.

Our attention to detail is second to none,
Our client's requirements remain number one.

We're the experts in our field,
And we'll turn your investments to give a good yield.

No fund is too large, no fund is too small,
If you need our help, then just give us a call.

But always heed these words of advice,
Whilst funds can go up, they can fall in a trice!

# RESPECT IS EVERYTHING!

Lord Bluff of Conmore lives down the road
With his wife and two kids in their 'humble' abode.

Each day you'll see them racing past
In their big flash machines, driving too fast!

There are two great big tractors, all shiny and green,
Covered in lights so they can be seen.

Get out of my way, don't you know who I am?
I'm a lordship you know, a very big man!

My ego's bigger than an elephant's bum
And the same can be said for that of my son.

I've snatched all the land from York through to home
And now there's not much that I do not own.

So get out of my way, and you'd better be quick,
Or I'll come down and drive you with my whipping stick!

But sire this road's closed, you cannot pass through.
In fact, this bit here doesn't belong to you.

But that's not right, how can this be?
I thought all this land belonged to me.

But sire I'm not lying, I tell you the truth.
This isn't part of an elaborate spoof.

You see, your father had fun when he was a lad,
Now he calls me son and I call him dad!

We're brothers you see, you must have known.
Now you'd better turn round and take yourself home.

But if I go round, it'll take me hours,
Perhaps I can use my persuasive powers?

You can keep your money, I'm not open to bribes.
For years I've put up with your hurtful jibes.

But I'm really sorry for this unfortunate spat,
I'm sure we can sort it with a beer and a chat.

You must be joking, you're far too late,
You should never have brought things to this desperate state.

But if I'd known who you were, we could have been mates,
Played tennis and golf and partied 'til late.

But that's where you're wrong, you're so underhand.
You see, a friend should be a friend from wherever you stand!

# MINT SAUCE AND WOOLLY JUMPERS

We've got issues with our sheep, they keep on getting out.
And when they do, it makes me cross and then I scream and shout!

"Come back you little blighters, don't run away from me,
'Cos when I finally get you home, we've got mint sauce for tea!"

But then we got the men with the fencing wire and stakes
To go round all the fields and block up all the gates.

So now you little sheepies, you can't just run away,
You've had your fun and games, and now you're here to stay.

But when I looked around again the rascals had all gone,
They'd only been and tunnelled out and now they're on the run!

And so I've finally given up owning any sheep,
I'm trying to think of something else that's not so hard to keep.

# RAGWORT AND BELLADONNA

Ragwort and Belladonna lived across the road,
He looked like a scarecrow and she just like a toad!

Ragwort and Belladonna lived on a farm,
Always spreading gossip, but said they meant no harm.

Yet on a daily basis outside they would be,
Telling tales about you just as huge as they could be.

The tales were very hurtful and mostly untrue,
But you had to stand and listen, there was nothing you could do.

Until one day they told a tale so twisted and perverted,
That in the tangle of the weave, it soon became inverted.

They became so rampant they had to be reported
And a man from MAFF came to get the problem sorted.

The spray he used was potent, they withered in the sun
And nothing has been seen of them since that deed was done!

While there's no harm in telling tales and having lots of fun,
If you overstep the mark then justice will be done.

So the moral of this story is to always tell the truth
And to always base your gossip on good old-fashioned proof!

# RURAL PURSUITS
### (Best sung to the tune of early one morning)

Early one morning, just as the sun was rising,
I spied my neighbour stalking in the garden below.
**What** is he doing there?
**What is** that in his hair?
Could it be the cow poo that was there a week ago?

# WHEN THE GOING GETS TOUGH

Stay strong, be brave and hang on to your dreams,
Try to look on the bright side despite how bad things seem.

# THE WALL IN OUR HALL

There is a wall in our hall
That needs a coat of paint.
My husband says he'll do it,
But it seems I'll have to wait.

I'd like to hang my poems
So everyone can see,
What Ali from the office
Truly thinks of me.

She really is quite cutting
And very often rude.
And some of what she writes about
Can put you off your food!

When all is said and done though,
It's fairly true to say,
That the poems do reflect me
In very many ways.

Yes I'm getting older,
My memory's gone to pot.
I do get very gassy
And I fart an awful lot!

But woe betide you Ali,
It's just a matter of time . . .
Before I get you back
With my own little rhyme!

## PLEASE RECYCLE ME

And if this book is not for you,
Don't throw it in the bin.
Please pass it on to someone else,
You just might make them grin!

# FAREWELL

And so the time has finally come
For me to say goodbye.
I can't do this in person
Because I know I'll cry.

I wanted to say thank you
For putting up with me.
I know it's not been easy
But now you'll all be free!

And thank you for all your help
In those times of need.
For giving me the strength to face
All my daily deeds.

And now I must move on,
There's so much to be done.
I wish you all the best there is
In all that's yet to come.